Cedric Wright

WORDS *of the* EARTH

. . . Were you thinking that those were the words, those upright lines?
          those curves, angles, dots?
No, those are not the words, the substantial words are in the ground and sea,
They are in the air, they are in you . . .
The workmanship of souls is by those inaudible words of the earth,
The masters know the earth's words and use them more than audible words . . .
To her children the words of the eloquent dumb great mother never fail . . .
Say on, sayers! Sing on, singers!
Delve! mould! pile the words of the earth!
Work on, age after age, nothing is to be lost,
It may have to wait long, but it will certainly come in use,
When the materials are all prepared and ready, the architects shall appear.

WALT WHITMAN

"A Song of the Rolling Earth"
Leaves of Grass

Edited by NANCY NEWHALL

Foreword by ANSEL ADAMS

CEDRIC WRIGHT:

Sierra Club • San Francisco

WORDS

of the EARTH

Library of Congress Catalog Number: 60–53176

Designed by Nancy Newhall and David Brower. Set in Centaur.
Composition by the Gillick Press, Berkeley. Gravure plates and
printing by Photogravure and Color Company, New York City.
Text Paper is Warren's Offset Enamel Dull. Cover stock is Curtis
Paper Company's Tweedweave. Binding by Russell-Rutter Company.

The Sierra Club, founded in 1892 by John Muir, has devoted
itself to the study and protection of national scenic resources,
particularly those of mountain regions. Participation is invited
in the program to enjoy and preserve wilderness, wildlife,
forests, and streams. Address: Mills Tower, San Francisco.

Distributed by Alfred A. Knopf, Publisher of Borzoi Books

FOREWORD

When confidence, intuition, humor, artistry, passionate ingenuity, and shyness function together in any one person we have an event of considerable importance. When we add to this galaxy of attributes the qualities of kindness and belief in the ultimate creative association of man and nature, we have a truly extraordinary situation. Such was Cedric Wright. He was no stylist in the usual sense of the term; he photographed and wrote tirelessly about what he felt deeply and truly believed. He was not concerned with the sophisticated adjustments of idea and impulse typical of the self-conscious artists of our time. Nature spoke simply and directly to him and he replied in similar vein. He was, in truth, an evangelist of special persuasion and compassion.

Above the complex emotional patterns of his life—which centered about the kaleidoscopically active days in Berkeley and the High Sierra—towers an edifice of beauty and imagination, a product of an uncompromising faith in nature and in people, things and experiences of great diversity. His work reveals a strange and compelling beauty; it is not obscure, oblique, mechanical, or intellectual, but is the evidence of a great insight and intuitive power. It moves the spirit; then, because it is so simple and direct, it moves the mind and conscience.

Twelve years my senior, Cedric Wright gave me confidence and support in many aspects of life, love, and the pursuit of individualism. He never "influenced" people in the ordinary sense of the term; he affirmed and clarified all valid experience. He firmly believed that "to know all is to forgive all." He had an uncanny awareness and distrust of the futilities, degenerations, and opportunisms encountered so frequently in contemporary music, graphic arts, literature, and photography. Over the years, Wright held fast to his own dream, selecting here and there, from all art expressions available to him, the statements necessary to the structure of his own creative life. He never expressed doubt or suffered introspections about the significance of his work, nor did he strive to associate it with the modes and manners of the world about him. His esthetic and communicative codes are to be found in Whitman, Edward Carpenter, H. G. Wells, Bach, and Beethoven—men who thought, wrote, composed, and lived in the fresh air of imagination, compassion, and understanding. Superficially, his philosophy may seem at times a confusion of ethics, mysticism, and blind faith, but in the end a pattern emerges which explains and justifies his intense creative compulsions. Elbert Hubbard gave him in his youth a gentle but often satirical attitude toward humanity and its manifestations of ego. Trained as a violinist, and gravitating to photography in his middle years, he always found it difficult to adapt himself to the configurations of formal and academic procedures. Nevertheless, he was an excellent teacher, imparting a sense of structure and intense emotional content, rather than expositions of conventional concepts and style. Fritz Kreisler, as a performing artist, was his ideal, and profoundly influenced his approach to music and photography. He had small taste for the mere virtuoso, and little regard for mechanics and style unless directly associated with emotional expression. His approach to photography was almost entirely empirical, yet the scope of his work was enormous—landscape and natural details, people and portraits, architecture and, as few realize, a massive body of technical work accomplished as photographer for the Radiation Laboratory in Berkeley during World War II. Granted his techniques were sometimes inconsistent, his photography always carries the stamp of his very particular personal vision.

One aspect of Wright's personality—memorable to his friends but extremely difficult to present out of the context of direct experience—was his egregious sense of humor. Frequently we discover this humor in his photography; it exhibits a sensitive and buoyant appreciation of the ridiculous, a rounding out of a gently applied comment on the human characteristics of people, things, and situations. It was this quality that provided the essential alleviations, balancing the severe and evangelical compulsions of his philosophy and effort. He was an unconscious master of dialect, and professed a unique concept of spelling and expressive rhetoric. Many of his letters contain the lilt of humor and the sheer excitement of life interest. Others are profoundly moving declarations of spirit and purpose. Throughout all his statements runs the firm thread of personality, binding his ideals, experiences, and friends into a pattern of comforting validity.

I write this little sketch not as a resumé of a deep, thirty-five year friendship, or as a definitive critique of his creative functions and accomplishment, but in the spirit of an earnest invitation to all who read this book to give more than a pleasurable survey of this tangible evidence of devotion and spirit. It is true that Cedric employed symbols to explain symbols—but what more can art in any form accomplish? The mood and actuality of a crisp Sierra dawn over a glittering meadow should be experienced by all our people—living here in the shadow of the Sierra as well as in the labyrinths of Chicago and New York. Towering granite peaks and rolling thunderclouds over a high-mountain lake are part of our basic heritage; many of the trapped urban millions may find it difficult to gain direct experience of wild places, but the creative intensity of art can bring them some of the magic and mystery of nature and encourage them to think, to dream, and perhaps to explore. The realities and bounties of nature are as actual as the urban and rural realities of our society, and may be recognized as such and accepted when experienced directly, or through some intense creative-emotional interpretations. Cedric believed that any man's spiritual horizon would be expanded through contact with nature, and his life was dedicated to this idea.

Many "realistic" and concrete-cultured critics scorn any simple exposition of natural beauty and wonder. To them, man is here to dominate the earth, not to live with it. Photographers of the hard-boiled journalistic school (usually steeped in the juices of discontent, disillusionment, and metropolitan survival techniques) avoid images of intrinsic mystical quality, and might not know a songful image if they saw it. Cedric Wright was in a constant cold war with such concrete and hard-boiled notions, and with the academic, business, and political conservatives. He had little use for the self-protective conventional wisdoms. He paid a price to live with his convictions, but it kept his genius intact and lost him none of the affection of his friends.

What is offered here is not merely a collection of nostalgic and beautiful pictures and poetic text, but a profound revelation of a most uncommon man, who, despite avalanches of problems and distractions, held fast to the essential dream. I regret there must be a date on this work because, in essence, it is timeless. Only the fact that it is concerned with photography places it in the relatively narrow confines of our age. With amazing clarity of appreciation and insight, Nancy Newhall has extracted from a tremendous sheaf of Cedric's writings the essence of his poetic vision, and has blended it with his photographs as equivalents of mood and meaning. And the Sierra Club affirms its aims and achievements in presenting this book as a memorial to one of its most illustrious spirits.

ANSEL ADAMS

San Francisco
August 20, 1960

CEDRIC WRIGHT, 1889–1959

PHOTOGRAPH BY ANSEL ADAMS

CREDO

. . . of composition, the most important considerations remain—to try to cover the
relationship of photography to our serious reactions to nature. In attempting this, it will be hard
to avoid making a noise like an oracle. One is translating from one language to another.
Rock, clouds, water, fire, in all their aura of light and sound and depth, must be brought into the
language—the materials—of a photographic print. For this, both languages must be
thoroughly felt and understood. This begins to be possible only when one's range of dynamics and
tones is that of a full-scale keyboard, and at the fingertips. Only then is photography an ample
voice, a resonant language . . .

A secret of fine results is to enjoy the most luxurious deliberation in each step of the work.
There is a contagious contentment about such an attitude, out of which is apt to flow more of the
spirit and qualities needed. Ideally it should be as if on that one part of the work alone were
focussed the entire essence of a lifetime . . .

I know a great architect whose style seems to have grown up through him out of the soil of his
environment. I have read a poet who reiterates over and over the value of the words of the earth.
Bernard Maybeck and Walt Whitman are the kind of authority for faith in the words of the earth.
This was Beethoven's faith.

Serious mountain photography must be evolved from such a faith. In these times photography

13

need not stand as a thing in itself, but may claim to be one of the ways toward a closeness with those remote voices, singing of a contented oneness in the world.

The artist will value *qualities* above what are usually considered *meanings*. Sunshine to the factual individual may be just sunshine. Sunshine to the dreamer may be a symbolical and wondrous thing. The smallest blade of grass or line of cloud may carry to one type of person, in some faint visionary way, the magic of its unknown life. A weathered timberline tree is a tremendous expression . . .

The mountain photographer is interpreting the face of nature—that mysterious infinity; eternally a refuge, a reservoir, an amplifier of the spirit, a mother of dreams, a positive though elusive voice in whose depth lies its subtle power. Those who interpret best are never so content as when under the influence of mountain surroundings, where silence is rich in mute assurance and beauty. Here the quality of emotional knowing is most clear . . .

Great art is usually created under some such saturation of awareness, where the work is permeated with an inner perception of beauty and an inner personal philosophy. So, the hope for our photography is that it shall retain high lights of more than beauty. That through it, symbols shall be preserved of response to our mountains, keeping them to flow, a golden thread in experience.

from "Mountain Photography,"
Sierra Club Bulletin, February 1941

CONTENTS

Have you ever watched a small white cloud dissolve
        into a background of blue space?
My search is for the kind of consciousness which could do just *that*
        to the causes of world friction.

We have been lost within sterile horizons.

Psychic forces know no boundaries.
To understand the relationships and currents tying together
   the whole creation,
      we must use the whole horizon of consciousness.

We need an education of the heart and spirit.
The most important things belong *first*, not last, or never.

In search of a new world, the wings of the spirit must not be clipped.

From time immemorial, the universe of the subconscious

    has been known most clearly in the wilderness—

    a universe of whose qualities and meanings words are faint symbols.

The insight of great creators penetrates the superstructure of consciousness.

Can those of us who have this arrow in our being be neutral?

A sound arises out of the earth—
a singing, a friendliness.

There is mighty contagion in the qualities of things—
    primitive and authentic joy in closeness
    to vital running water, fire, wind,

vast integrity in real experience of the earth, the stars,
subtle and dynamic wonder in peak and cloud.

An inquiry now, into the roots of our being.

What is sanity?

Sometimes it seems as if only things like blades of grass have sanity—
     as if only through their serenity, their mute virtue and wisdom,
     could we gain a sense of life as it might become.

Generations have dimly felt that somehow within nature lies a template
     for guidance—
     that genuine revelation lies within the livingness of grass,
          of cloud, of light—
     a revelation sharpening our knowing of the roots of kindness,
          the beginnings of humility.

One foot of beach sand: see it, feel it.
Search out its lines, its arrangements,
  its acceptance of inevitables,
    of destiny in the laws of gravity and of light reflection.

A glistening silent world.
Imagine all that must be happening there, beyond our knowing.

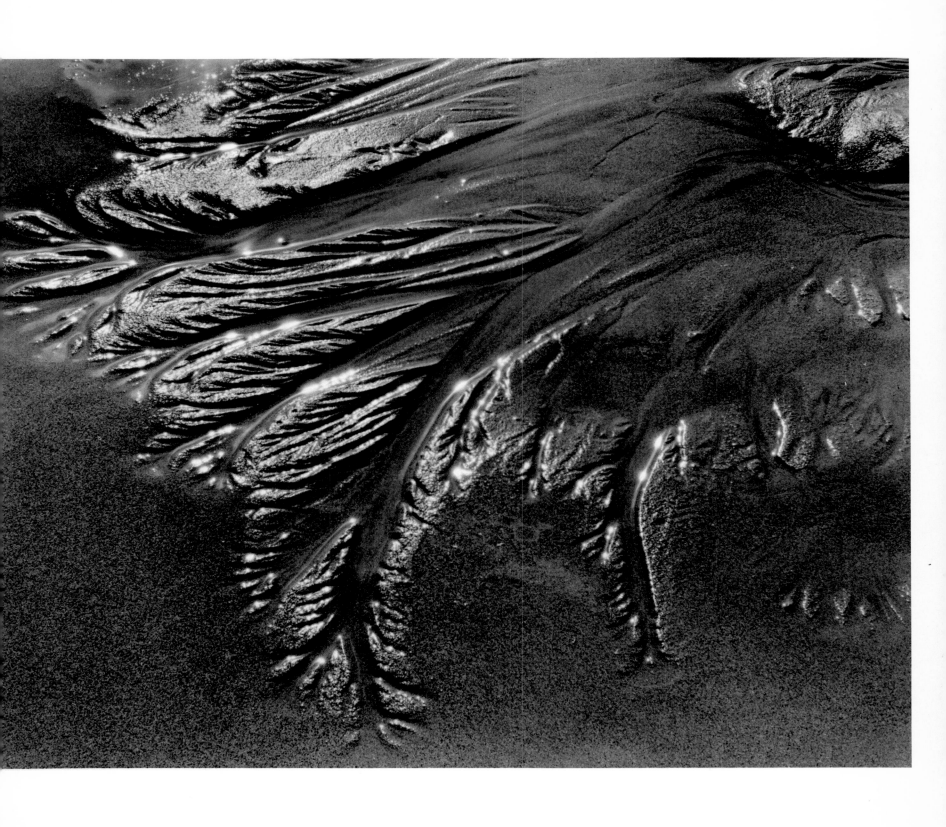

A match, lit out of the wind in the cup of the hand,
      survives most surely if tilted sharply down
      and slowly revolved when kindled.
The same thing happens to kindling twigs—resinous twigs, picked
      not off the ground, but from the slender tips of dead tree branches,
      and broken to desired length by tapping over a boulder.
These should be held in the hand like a bouquet pointing downward until
      they blaze, then laid on the ground, and twigs of increasing size
      added at varying angles—never parallel, lest you smother the flames.
Now set your can of water on flat earth or coals, and tuck small twigs
      about it—small twigs caress your billycan.
Fire should be concentrated to windward—away from the side to be grabbed—
      and if your billycan has a handle of bailing wire, a lifting stick
      made ready.
And, as soon as the precious hot water is poured into wash basin and cup,
      a second batch is put on to heat.
For what? Why, to get places socially!
      The arrival of free hot water is one of the most potent social entrees
      in the camping world—especially if you give your first batch away!
I find this gentle puttering, making an art of a billycan fire,
      more fun than any game.
But the praise of billycan fires and humble generosity
      has never been sufficiently sung.

Firelighting stretches past frontier days into archaic vistas.
There is a long history of man and fire.
Something from the past descends
    and flows down silently on firewatchers,
      like the dim racial memory of rain.

Untrammelled, a roving spirit responds to faint implication and symbol—
    to the fall of rain.
In time of rain, the archaic being stirs.
The infinity of soft sounds, the silken pervasion of falling water,
    distills a love of shelter, fireside, home, sweet air, greenness,
    timelessness, renewal.
All these belong to the gentleness of rain
    and the flow and benediction after rain.

Trouble is a fierce rain that drives us to the shelter of our friends.
And there is the rain of tears,
    distilling the memory of great love and its expansiveness,
    making of rain an inner light, a subtle possession of the spirit.

Consider the life of trees.

Aside from the axe, what trees acquire from man is inconsiderable.

What man may acquire from trees is immeasurable.

From their mute forms there flows a poise, in silence,

    a lovely sound and motion in response to wind.

What peace comes to those aware of the voice and bearing of trees!

Trees do not scream for attention.

A tree, a rock, has no pretence, only a real growth out of itself,

    in close communion with the universal spirit.

A tree retains a deep serenity.

It establishes in the earth not only its root system but also those roots

    of its beauty and its unknown consciousness.

Sometimes one may sense a glisten of that consciousness, and with such

    perspective, feel that man is not necessarily the highest form of life.

Tree qualities, after long communion, come to reside in man.
As stillness enhances sound, so through little things
     the joy of living expands.
One is aware, lying under trees,
     of the roots and directions of one's whole being.
Perceptions drift in from earth and sky.
A vast healing begins.

The days of our lives must become precious.

In all heaven and earth, there is this one thing to do:
    take your time.
Enjoy the perfection of what you are doing.
Enjoy accomplishing it exquisitely.

Human life must know ecstasy.

I take my mountains as music.
The mountains wake a singing undercurrent,
    then overtones,
    then sing with you.

Music haunts the high country like a hymn,
    floats in the cold sunny air
    moulds the clouds
    filtering those floods of light and shadow
    that forever clothe the mountains anew —
Stop and listen to the birds on these high ridges!
O, to emulate this mountain music!

Music arrives in the deep hum
        of river and wind through the forest,
        speaks through wave-lines in sunlight
        and in shimmer of wind rippling—
        until we too fuse with it,
        fairly humming its key and clef,
        swelling the chorus, joining its universal breadth.

We crossed the pass on a day of thunder.

Cloud tunnels into the far reaches of space
revealed an unearthly design and motion,
and a towering resonance filled the canyons.

From here we must go down, down ten thousand feet,
        down to accustomed levels,
        down to the blare and cry of ordinary living.

From within the sounds and banners of the vast horizon,

    without words, into an inner silence, came:

    Remember well this magnitude.

    Lift your eyes,

        that the great meanings shall not flow by unheeded.

    See.

    The world's beauty carries in trust

        the importance of your salvation.

To some who think themselves wise, mountains are piles of dirt.
To them, science and the microscope reveal the wilderness to be
      a record of struggle and failure,
      a battleground to the death.
And they conclude that our main concern,
      under the same unalterable laws,
      is to prepare for a life and death struggle.

Yet the aggression of weeds against flowers, if left alone,
   creates a balance and fitness.
Within each species lies its destiny,
   its place in the wilderness economy and order.
Where do flowers look so well as when left to natural law?

Design of deep momentums—
Trees tragic, trees broken by winter, trees in all stages of decay,
dead branches and pine needles strewn upon the snow,
    in patterns dictated by subtle law:
    of wind, gravitation, carefree instinct.

Yet each fallen bough, each dead stump,
intensifies the richness of the forest.

Out of the vast process of evolution through need,
        out of the cycle of passing forms,
        arises eternal, elemental beauty.

Intense beauty is liberation.

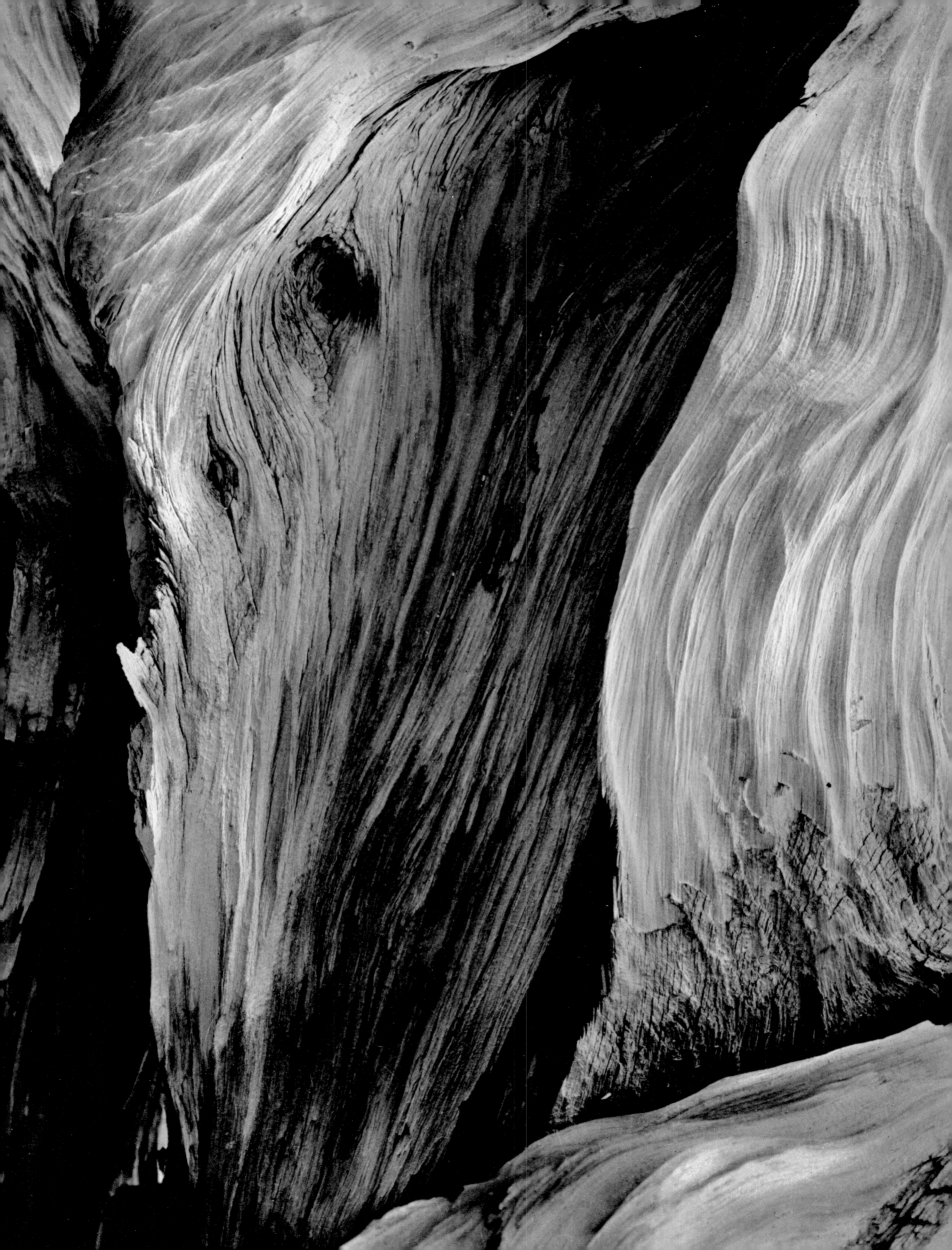

Here again, as everywhere,
    the great river passing—
    I passing,
    you passing . . .

. . . forever flowing down through time,
   flowing through many channels,
   fading out of the embraces of its names . . .

. . . simple as the voice of a child
and never to be quite known.

In this light and breeze are resurrection echoes.

Suddenly one becomes aware one lives in an eternity,
and hears strange footsteps
ascending anciently trodden pathways.

Consciousness projects itself
    like a headland into the seas.
Headlands acquire sea atmosphere;
    headlands are poised
        in the sound of waves,
    headlands extend
        in long dreaming lines of shore.
From the unknown,
    from the immense and infinite,
    weaving into consciousness
        like long fingers of fog
        through coastal canyons,
    comes a far-off singing.

Out of the sea, in vast currents,
    a mystic essence arises—
    essence of the infinite godliness
    which creates worlds.

A new astronomy of the spirit
    should become a conscious goal of man.

Our lives like dreams endure
      and reach out over the universe.
Nothing real is to itself alone.
There are sidestreams to rivers; there are overtones to thought.
Great love reaches out
      and is involved in the world's purposes.

Our loves are only symbols of an unknown immortality.
Where communion is deep, there exists no separation at all,
    for what needs telling those we love is understood already,
    and what is supposed to be gone and past
        is often more real than ever.
Through the sculpture of experience,
    that part of ourselves which survives,
    like cloud, resolves continuously.
This is the spirit of my hope and my religion.

Love and the loss of love,
        the loss of life, frustrations in one's hopes, birth—
        to each of us these are mysteries.
Through these come love and pity for the world's misery
        and a sustained wonder at the long-range continuity
                underrunning all events, all material things,
                rooted in a spiritual universe.
Faith in a deep purpose dawns.

There are days when a high cold wind races out of space,
     the space of stars.
Within vast vistas, one feels alone.
In such solitude, true religion is born.

From these mountains and cloud haloes
        ascend eternal meanings.
A great world music floods consciousness.
A larger love flows into living,
        from which vast and subtle change
        shall descend upon the nations,
        bringing healing.

PUBLISHER'S
NOTE

ON A PAGE he wrote in 1954 to preface one of the many early versions of *Words of the Earth,* Cedric Wright said: "I have been unusually privileged in knowing intimately those wilderness areas where the intangible values sing clearly. It has seemed important to conserve the significance of that singing, to understand its significance not merely in some art form, but rather to try to clarify what it could bring to human life in general. The artist seeks fundamental beauty, the voice of concord, in a world which is presently dominated by opposite types of understanding. Beauty and understanding are the foundations not only of art, but also of a peaceful human world. It is imperative that in such times as these the artist should use his words and his thought in addition to his art."

With the sensitive aid of Nancy Newhall, Wright has posthumously made an integral whole of words, thought, and art. How all this could happen is a long story that I think will have to be told one day, when people seek out the beginnings of the beauty in this book. But for now, I'd like to start merely with my recollection that in the summer of 1953, at a camp high on the Kern, Cedric told me that this was his thirty-third High Trip (the eleventh we had shared)—which is to say that he had spent almost three years of summer days on the species of Sierra Club outing that has taken people of widely ranging means far back into big wilderness, mostly in the Sierra Nevada, since 1901. All too soon after that camp there was a sad task, an obituary to write for the November 1959 *Sierra Club Bulletin,* that said this:

*   *   *   *   *   *

IN THE HIGH SIERRA wilderness country that is the climax of what John Muir liked to call the Range of Light, Wright fell in love with the high world even as Muir had, and each summer brought him closer to its forms, its moods, its tones, its light—and to the thousand textures that unfolded as the trail turned or as a trailless slope opened up on a broad sweep or an intimate glen that no man had seen before.

Oh, others may have stood there, yes. But none could see what he saw, not until with black cloth and box he had worked his magic, had captured and carried away the essence of beauty without harming a hair of it, had printed and fixed its image, had let others see it at last, far from where it was, and had led them, in that way, to look for it and find it next time.

On many of these high trips Wright served as official photographer, meaning that the check he sent in for a reservation on the trip was returned to him in gratitude for what he had already contributed, worth many times a trip's cost, in exquisite display prints of the previous year's trip. These became the mainstay of the club's permanent photographic collection; they were augmented by Wright's gift to the club of all his Sierra negatives.

From these prints and negatives will come the illustrations for Cedric Wright's book which the Sierra Club plans to publish as a memorial next year, "Words of the Earth"—the High Sierra earth. The text comes from the same piece of terrain. People who knew Wright in his mountains—and there are hundreds who did—know that the text came to him by osmosis as he lay upon some choice piece of Sierra, in between his exposures of film, and was himself exposed to inaudible words and music. The book will contain the best of his poetic expression and of his photographs. It will be of fairly large format to let the photographs be big enough to speak clearly, and they will be reproduced just as handsomely as present-day achievements in graphic arts will permit. To aid this major project and to widen the audience for his artistry, the club is accepting, with Rhea Wright's permission, donations to a Cedric Wright Memorial Fund.

One of the nicest of all memorials to Cedric Wright, however, is the picture so many friends carry in their mind's eye of Cedric before the first of a series of strokes grounded him and impaired his eyesight. For in that picture he is the Good Samaritan of the trailside, bringing music to a campfire, pouring a warming cup of tea from his billy-can for the weary traveler, brightening the tired end of a day with his good humor and his good heart. Above all, we his friends are grateful that because he saw clearly, we can begin to see clearly, or at least be less unseeing.

*   *   *   *   *   *

AS A POSTSCRIPT, we should share with you two of the notes written on odd-sized pieces of paper, that turned up in the vast collection of splendid negatives. One says:

"*Explanation of my filing system.* All the best negatives from over 3 or 4 years past are in this box. Recent years' negatives have been left in the straw basket—each High Trip, 1949 on—in packings by themselves. It might be well to give all my negatives to the Sierra Club."

And the other:

"It's been beyond me, to figure out how to file all my negatives intelligently. Most all my portrait negatives are in the cellar in fruit boxes."

It has been almost beyond the Sierra Club, too. All friends who hold this book should also hold themselves in readiness for an emergency call from the Sierra Club to attend a gigantic identification party, to pass and review all the examples of evanescent beauty that Cedric stopped and fixed, and to tell us, while human memory still can, where he was at the time, and what or whom he was photographing!

DAVID BROWER
Executive Director
Sierra Club

PHOTOGRAPHS